COMPOSER
SHOWCASE
HAL LEONARD
STUDENT PIANO LIBRARY

Magical OVERTURES

10 EXCITING PIANO SOLOS
BY DENNIS ALEXANDER

ISBN 978-1-70514-328-5

HAL•LEONARD®

Visit Hal Leonard Online at
www.halleonard.com

Contact us:
Hal Leonard
7777 West Bluemound Road
Milwaukee, WI 53213
Email: info@halleonard.com

In Europe, contact:
Hal Leonard Europe Limited
42 Wigmore Street
Marylebone, London, W1U 2RN
Email: info@halleonardeurope.com

In Australia, contact:
Hal Leonard Australia Pty. Ltd.
4 Lentara Court
Cheltenham, Victoria, 3192 Australia
Email: info@halleonard.com.au

Performance Notes

Panache!

The definition of panache is: "flamboyant confidence of style or manner." Consequently, this piece needs to be played with lots of spirit and energy! Be sure to shape all of the rapid 5-note and 3-note phrases with emphasis on the first note, while lifting out of the ending of each phrase with a rising wrist staccato motion. Start m. 17 softly, with a dramatic crescendo to the end! And give that last note in the LH a nice, dramatic closing gesture.

Une Petite Valse

This short waltz is an excellent study for developing beautiful legato between the hands, while also achieving a variety of articulation. Be careful to avoid accenting beat 3, and place the emphasis on the half-note downbeats. Notice that the three strongest fingers play together on the parallel motion legato patterns in mm. 3-4 and throughout this piece.

The Royal Couple

Pretend that this RH melody is a trumpet fanfare, announcing the arrival of a royal couple! Observe the staccato markings in the RH against the legato half notes in the LH. Again, the strongest fingers in each hand (3-2-1) will help to make this easier to perform with confidence. The open fifths in the middle section (as well as ending) help to ensure a solid, rounded hand position. Play the last two measures with the full arm to create a rich, big sound.

Copycats

This is an excellent piece to develop the concept of *counterpoint*, so critical when playing Baroque music. Careful attention to fingering and articulation will give this piece the clarity and stylistic qualities that are needed.

Lydian March

Built on the Lydian scale (raised 4th), this is a great piece to help students achieve a full, rich sound! For those opening fifths in the LH, use weight from the upper arm behind the fingers to create a nice big sound. As soon as the sound is made, relax the wrist, floating back and forth from register to register. Be sure to start m. 31 softly with each succeeding measure growing in intensity to the final *ff* in m. 34.

Creepers!

This one is designed to help students bring out a LH melodic line, while keeping the accompanying chords in the RH softer. It's also an opportunity for students to explore chromatic patterns in both hands. There are lots of dynamic changes that will embolden the drama and really bring this piece to life!

Perilous Journey

Students will enjoy the suspense within this solo—created by the mysterious sounds, rhythms, variety of articulations, and clashing harmonies of loud polytonal triads, combined with the pedal. It's bound to be a crowd pleaser on any recital program.

Gotta Boogie Woogie!

Filled with high energy, syncopation, LH crossing over RH, and boogie-woogie character, this motivational piece will help a performer achieve speed and dexterity. Isolating m. 13 and m. 17 and drilling this pattern multiple times will help to instill confidence and control! Give the whole-note in m. 33 full value before playing the last note in the LH so as to add to the drama of this rollicking piece.

Lys flottants

It's always fun to find an impressionistic style piece at this level. Play more on the pads of the fingers throughout this short work, always listening for the colors of sound needed to help convey the impression of lilies floating on a gentle lake or pond. Use pedal only where indicated.

Synergy

Students looking for a high energy, driving piece that sounds harder than it actually is will have lots of fun performing this work! Open fifths in each hand abound, and the mixed meters, accents, and boundless energy will make this solo really shine.

Preface

The word *overture* has been defined as "an introduction to something more substantial." My Overture series for piano solo is just that!

Magical Overtures is the second book of three, and you'll find a mix of pieces that will motivate and inspire. They are perfect for auditions, festivals, or recitals. Mixed meters, Lydian mode, Impressionistic, Romantic, Contemporary, Boogie Woogie—it's all here. Each piece contains technical and musical challenges, from lyrical melodic styles to fast rhythmical pieces. In addition, almost every solo in this book works well for those with smaller hands who want something that sounds "impressive."

Enjoy these pieces, and may they be an introduction to more substantial works in your musical journey!

Dennis Alexander
July 2021

Contents

Panache!

Dennis Alexander

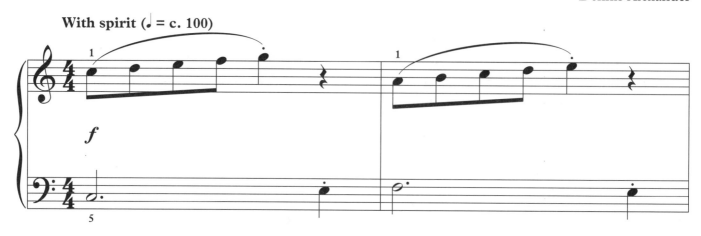

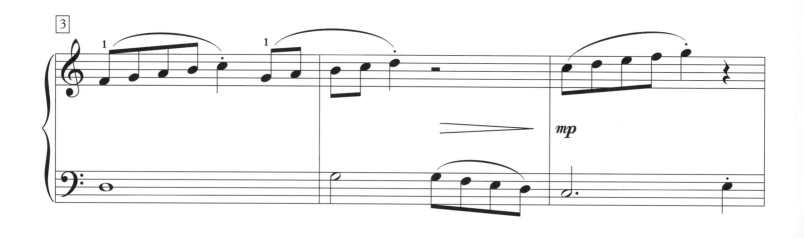

Une Petite Valse

Dennis Alexander

Moderato (♩ = c. 124)

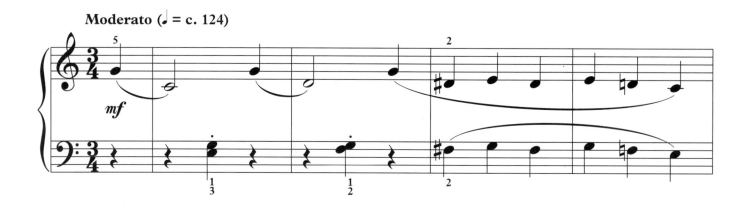

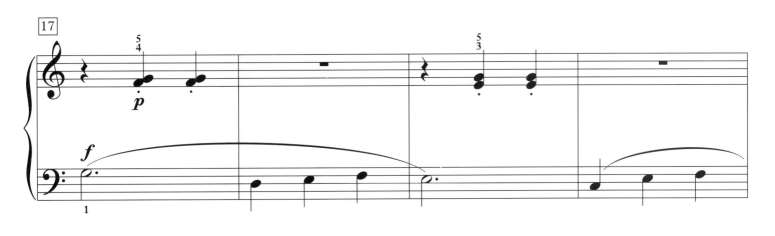

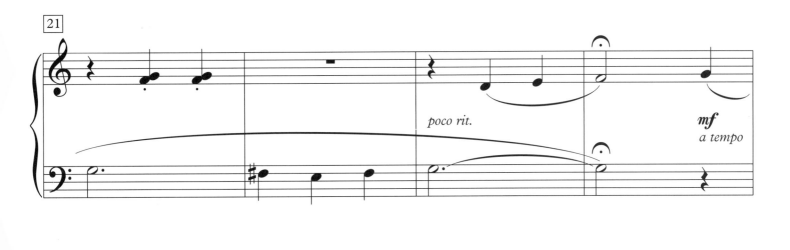

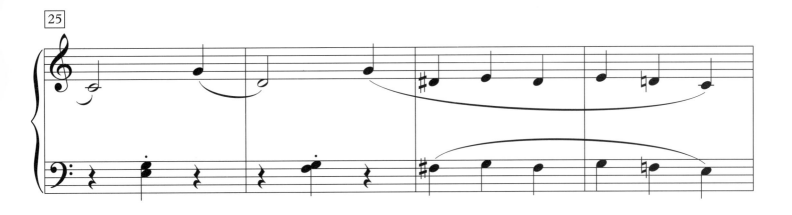

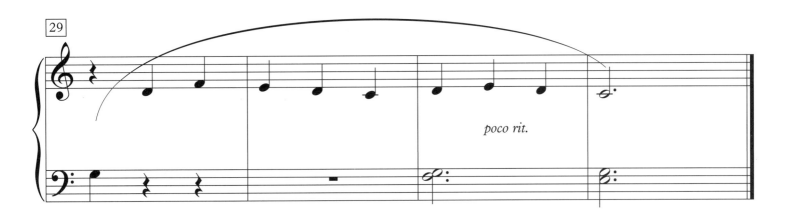

The Royal Couple

Dennis Alexander

Copycats

Dennis Alexander

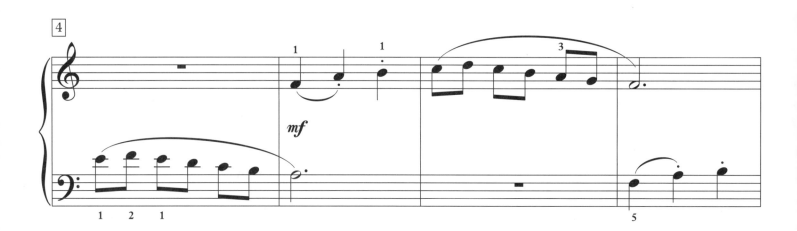

Lydian March

Dennis Alexander

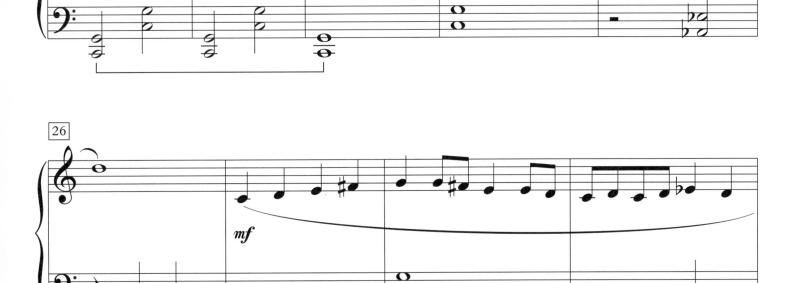

Creepers!

Dennis Alexander

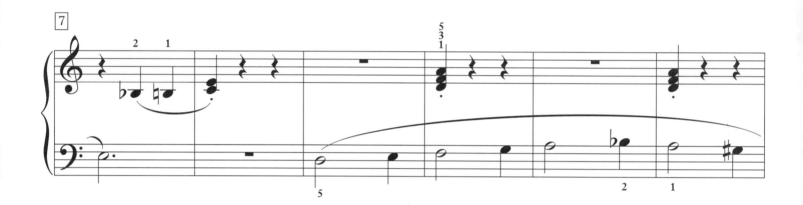

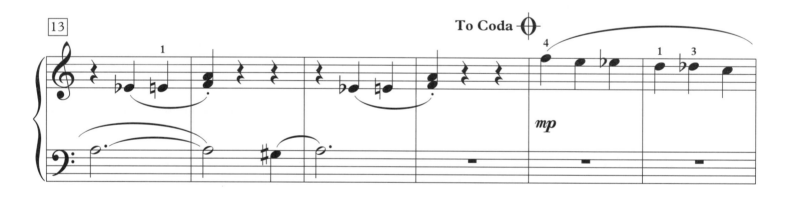

Perilous Journey

Dennis Alexander

Gotta Boogie Woogie!

Dennis Alexander

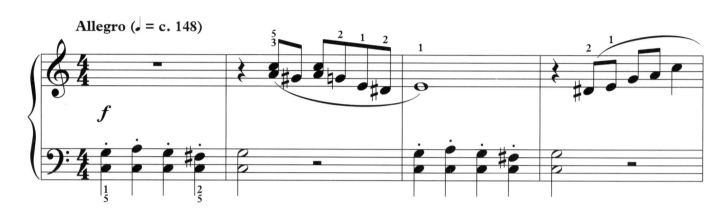

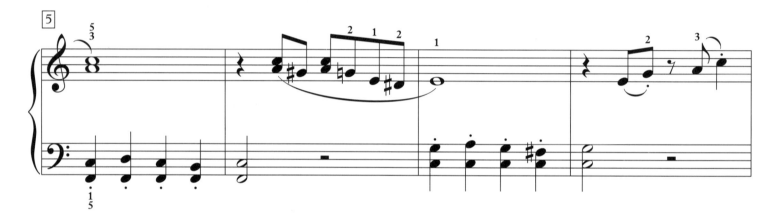

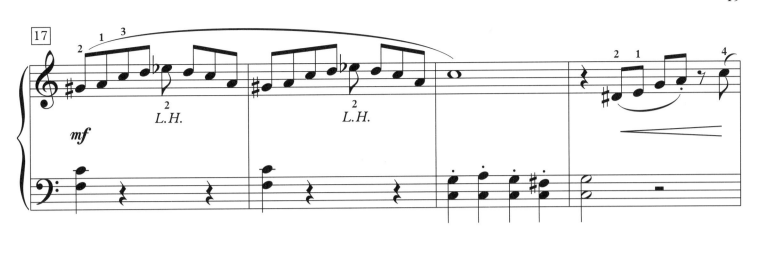

Lys flottants
(Floating lilies)

Dennis Alexander

Gently (♩. = c. 106)

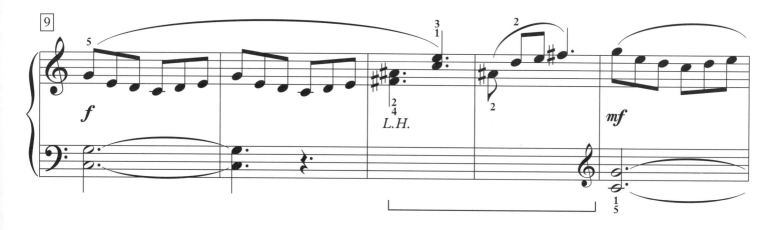

Synergy

Dennis Alexander

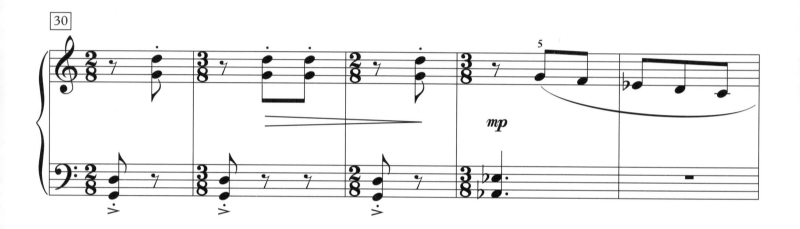

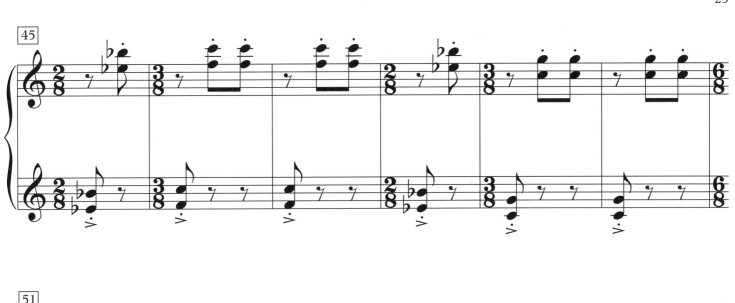

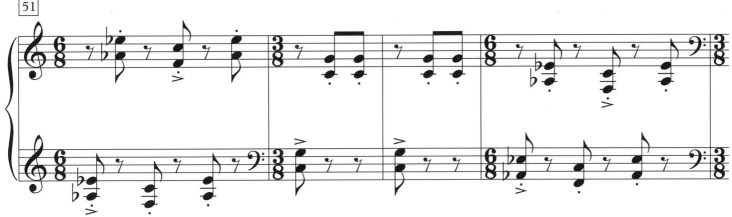

This series showcases great original piano music from our **Hal Leonard Student Piano Library** family of composers. Carefully graded for easy selection.

BILL BOYD

JAZZ BITS (AND PIECES)
Early Intermediate Level
00290312 11 Solos......................$7.99

JAZZ DELIGHTS
Intermediate Level
00240435 11 Solos......................$8.99

JAZZ FEST
Intermediate Level
00240436 10 Solos......................$8.99

JAZZ PRELIMS
Early Elementary Level
00290032 12 Solos......................$7.99

JAZZ SKETCHES
Intermediate Level
00220001 8 Solos......................$8.99

JAZZ STARTERS
Elementary Level
00290425 10 Solos......................$8.99

JAZZ STARTERS II
Late Elementary Level
00290434 11 Solos......................$7.99

JAZZ STARTERS III
Late Elementary Level
00290465 12 Solos......................$8.99

THINK JAZZ!
Early Intermediate Level
00290417 Method Book............$12.99

TONY CARAMIA

JAZZ MOODS
Intermediate Level
00296728 8 Solos......................$6.95

SUITE DREAMS
Intermediate Level
00296775 4 Solos......................$6.99

SONDRA CLARK

DAKOTA DAYS
Intermediate Level
00296521 5 Solos......................$6.95

FLORIDA FANTASY SUITE
Intermediate Level
00296766 3 Duets......................$7.95

THREE ODD METERS
Intermediate Level
00296472 3 Duets......................$6.95

MATTHEW EDWARDS

CONCERTO FOR YOUNG PIANISTS
FOR 2 PIANOS, FOUR HANDS
Intermediate Level Book/CD
00296356 3 Movements $19.99

CONCERTO NO. 2 IN G MAJOR
FOR 2 PIANOS, 4 HANDS
Intermediate Level Book/CD
00296670 3 Movements............$17.99

PHILLIP KEVEREN

MOUSE ON A MIRROR
Late Elementary Level
00296361 5 Solos......................$8.99

MUSICAL MOODS
Elementary/Late Elementary Level
00296714 7 Solos......................$6.99

SHIFTY-EYED BLUES
Late Elementary Level
00296374 5 Solos......................$7.99

CAROL KLOSE

THE BEST OF CAROL KLOSE
Early to Late Intermediate Level
00146151 15 Solos....................$12.99

CORAL REEF SUITE
Late Elementary Level
00296354 7 Solos......................$7.50

DESERT SUITE
Intermediate Level
00296667 6 Solos......................$7.99

FANCIFUL WALTZES
Early Intermediate Level
00296473 5 Solos......................$7.95

GARDEN TREASURES
Late Intermediate Level
00296787 5 Solos......................$8.50

ROMANTIC EXPRESSIONS
Intermediate to Late Intermediate Level
00296923 5 Solos......................$8.99

WATERCOLOR MINIATURES
Early Intermediate Level
00296848 7 Solos......................$7.99

JENNIFER LINN

AMERICAN IMPRESSIONS
Intermediate Level
00296471 6 Solos......................$8.99

ANIMALS HAVE FEELINGS TOO
Early Elementary/Elementary Level
00147789 8 Solos......................$8.99

AU CHOCOLAT
Late Elementary/Early Intermediate Level
00298110 7 Solos......................$8.99

CHRISTMAS IMPRESSIONS
Intermediate Level
00296706 8 Solos......................$8.99

JUST PINK
Elementary Level
00296722 9 Solos......................$8.99

LES PETITES IMAGES
Late Elementary Level
00296664 7 Solos......................$8.99

LES PETITES IMPRESSIONS
Intermediate Level
00296355 6 Solos......................$8.99

REFLECTIONS
Late Intermediate Level
00296843 5 Solos......................$8.99

TALES OF MYSTERY
Intermediate Level
00296769 6 Solos......................$8.99

LYNDA LYBECK-ROBINSON

ALASKA SKETCHES
Early Intermediate Level
00119637 8 Solos......................$8.99

AN AWESOME ADVENTURE
Late Elementary Level
00137563 8 Solos......................$7.99

FOR THE BIRDS
Early Intermediate/Intermediate Level
00237078 9 Solos......................$8.99

WHISPERING WOODS
Late Elementary Level
00275905 9 Solos......................$8.99

MONA REJINO

CIRCUS SUITE
Late Elementary Level
00296665 5 Solos......................$8.99

COLOR WHEEL
Early Intermediate Level
00201951 6 Solos......................$9.99

IMPRESIONES DE ESPAÑA
Intermediate Level
00337520 6 Solos......................$8.99

IMPRESSIONS OF NEW YORK
Intermediate Level
00364212.....................................$8.99

JUST FOR KIDS
Elementary Level
00296840 8 Solos......................$7.99

MERRY CHRISTMAS MEDLEYS
Intermediate Level
00296799 5 Solos......................$8.99

MINIATURES IN STYLE
Intermediate Level
00148088 6 Solos......................$8.99

PORTRAITS IN STYLE
Early Intermediate Level
00296507 6 Solos......................$8.99

EUGÉNIE ROCHEROLLE

CELEBRATION SUITE
Intermediate Level
00152724 3 Duets......................$8.99

ENCANTOS ESPAÑOLES (SPANISH DELIGHTS)
Intermediate Level
00125451 6 Solos......................$8.99

JAMBALAYA
Intermediate Level
00296654 2 Pianos, 8 Hands.....$12.99
00296725 2 Pianos, 4 Hands.......$7.95

JEROME KERN CLASSICS
Intermediate Level
00296577 10 Solos....................$12.99

LITTLE BLUES CONCERTO
Early Intermediate Level
00142801 2 Pianos, 4 Hands......$12.99

TOUR FOR TWO
Late Elementary Level
00296832 6 Duets......................$9.99

TREASURES
Late Elementary/Early Intermediate Level
00296924 7 Solos......................$8.99

JEREMY SISKIND

BIG APPLE JAZZ
Intermediate Level
00278209 8 Solos......................$8.99

MYTHS AND MONSTERS
Late Elementary/Early Intermediate Level
00148148 9 Solos......................$8.99

CHRISTOS TSITSAROS

DANCES FROM AROUND THE WORLD
Early Intermediate Level
00296688 7 Solos......................$8.99

FIVE SUMMER PIECES
Late Intermediate/Advanced Level
00361235 5 Solos....................$12.99

LYRIC BALLADS
Intermediate/Late Intermediate Level
00102404 6 Solos......................$8.99

POETIC MOMENTS
Intermediate Level
00296403 8 Solos......................$8.99

SEA DIARY
Early Intermediate Level
00253486 9 Solos......................$8.99

SONATINA HUMORESQUE
Late Intermediate Level
00296772 3 Movements............$6.99

SONGS WITHOUT WORDS
Intermediate Level
00296506 9 Solos......................$9.99

THREE PRELUDES
Early Advanced Level
00130747 3 Solos......................$8.99

THROUGHOUT THE YEAR
Late Elementary Level
00296723 12 Duets......................$6.95

ADDITIONAL COLLECTIONS

AT THE LAKE
by Elvina Pearce
Elementary/Late Elementary Level
00131642 10 Solos and Duets.....$7.99

CHRISTMAS FOR TWO
by Dan Fox
Early Intermediate Level
00290069 13 Duets......................$8.99

CHRISTMAS JAZZ
by Mike Springer
Intermediate Level
00296525 6 Solos......................$8.99

COUNTY RAGTIME FESTIVAL
by Fred Kern
Intermediate Level
00296882 7 Solos......................$7.99

LITTLE JAZZERS
by Jennifer Watts
Elementary/Late Elementary Level
00154573 9 Solos......................$8.99

PLAY THE BLUES!
by Luann Carman
Early Intermediate Level
00296357 10 Solos....................$9.99

ROLLER COASTERS & RIDES
by Jennifer & Mike Watts
Intermediate Level
00131144 8 Duets......................$8.99

HAL•LEONARD®

www.halleonard.com

Prices, contents, and availability subject to change without notice.

0321

144